TO BRITTANY

FROM SH...

JUNE 2010

Wisdom *for* Graduates

EDITED BY

ALISON BING

Wisdom *for* Graduates

Words to the Wise From

the Even Wiser

BARNES
& NOBLE
NEW YORK

Book design by Nicola Ferguson

2007 Barnes & Noble, Inc.

ISBN-13: 978-0-7607-9270-4
ISBN-10: 0-7607-9270-4

Printed and bound in the United States of America

10 9 8 7 6 5 4 3 2 1

Introduction

Congratulations, graduate!

Nice tassel you've got yourself there. That took some doing. Considering what you went through to get your degree, you ought to get some mileage out of it. Sadly, life offers you far fewer opportunities to flash your diploma than, say, a bus pass. Ironic, isn't it? Probably getting that bus pass didn't keep you up nights or require you to wear a square hat.

But before you go crying foul on life, know that there are more suave ways to work that diploma than toting around a mini laminated version in your wallet. Just quote a well-known thinker in a casual yet audible tone, and everyone within earshot will immediately recognize you as the learned graduate you are. So now whenever an opportunity to wax philosophical arises, you'll be waxing to a high shine.

Enjoy the book, and your accolades. You have them coming—you had the wisdom to buy this book, after all.

Sincerely,
Alison Bing,
about whom W. Somerset Maugham
once said: "She had a pretty gift for quotation, which
is a serviceable substitute for wit."

Learning

The Purpose of Education

It is part of the function of education to help us escape—not from our own time, for we are bound by that—but from the intellectual and emotional limitations of our own time.

—T. S. Eliot, poet

Education is an ornament in prosperity and a refuge in adversity.

—Aristotle, philosopher

Many men have been just as troubled morally and spiritually as you are right now. Happily, some of them kept records of their troubles. You'll learn from them—if you want to. Just as someday, if you have something to offer, someone will learn something from you. It's a beautiful reciprocal arrangement. And it isn't education. It's history. It's poetry.

—J.D. Salinger, writer

Human history becomes more and more a race between education and catastrophe.

—H.G.Wells, writer

Education is the passport to our future.

—Malcolm X, civil rights activist
and spiritual leader

He who opens a school door, closes a prison.

—*Victor Hugo, writer*

Education is when you read the fine print; experience is what you get when you don't.

—*Pete Seeger, musician and social activist*

Education is the ability to listen to almost anything without losing your temper or your self-confidence.

—*Robert Frost, poet*

Perhaps the most valuable result of all education is the ability to make yourself do the thing you have to do, when it ought to be done, whether you like it or not.

—*Thomas Huxley, scientist*

Education is not the filling of a pail, but the lighting of a fire.

—*William Butler Yeats, poet*

The mind is like a richly woven tapestry in which the colors are distilled from the experiences of the senses, and the design drawn from the convolutions of the intellect.

—*Carson McCullers, writer*

To think and to be fully alive are the same.

—*Hannah Arendt, philosopher*

A man is but the product of his thoughts. What he thinks, he becomes.

—*Mohandas K. Gandhi, politician and spiritual leader*

Teachers

If I have seen further than others, it is by stand-
ing on the shoulders of giants.

—Sir Isaac Newton, scientist

One looks back with appreciation to the brilliant teachers, but with gratitude to those who
touched our human feelings. The curriculum is
so much necessary new material, but warmth is
the vital element for the growing plant and for
the soul of the child.

—Carl Gustav Jung, psychiatrist

I am indebted to my father for living, but to my
teacher for living well.

—Alexander the Great, general and emperor

A professor is one who talks in someone else's sleep.

—W. H. Auden, poet

I have come to believe that a great teacher is a great artist and that there are as few as there are any other great artists. Teaching might even be the greatest of the arts, since the medium is the human mind and spirit.

—John Steinbeck, author

It is the supreme art of the teacher to awaken joy in creative expression and knowledge.

—Albert Einstein, physicist

I like a teacher who gives you something to take home to think about besides homework.

—*Lily Tomlin, comedian*

We cannot teach people anything; we can only help them discover it within themselves.

—*Galileo Galilei, astronomer*

...We hear the teachers
as if they were far off, speaking
down a tube. Sometimes
a whole sentence gets through.
But the teachers don't give up.
They rise, dress, appear before us
Crisp and hopeful. They have a plan.

—*Naomi Shihab Nye, poet*

Knowledge & Power

Knowledge is power.

—*Francis Bacon, philosopher*

The voice of the intellect is a soft one, but it does not rest till it has gained a hearing.

—*Sigmund Freud, psychiatrist*

There are no dangerous thoughts; thinking itself is dangerous.

—*Hannah Arendt, philosopher*

Education is the most powerful weapon you can use to change the world.

—*Nelson Mandela, former South African president*

If Virtue & Knowledge are diffus'd among the People, they will never be enslav'd. This will be their great Security.

—*Samuel Adams, politician*

If you think education is expensive, try ignorance.

—*Emma Goldman, social activist*

Educated Women

If we mean to have heroes, statesmen, and philosophers, we should have learned women.

—*Abigail Adams, writer*
and U.S. First Lady

How wrong it is for a woman to expect the man to build the world she wants, rather than to create it herself!

—*Anaïs Nin, writer*

I like a woman with a head on her shoulders. I hate necks.

—*Steve Martin, writer and comedian*

The presence on the stage of these college women, and in the audience of all those college girls who will someday be the nation's greatest strength, will tell their own story to the world.

—*Susan B. Anthony, women's rights activist*

Room for Improvement

You'll find that the only thing you can do easily is be wrong, and that's hardly worth the effort.

—*Norton Juster, writer*

Today's public figures can no longer write their own speeches or books, and there is some evidence that they can't read them either.

—*Gore Vidal, author*

There is an almost universal quest for easy answers and half-baked solutions. Nothing pains some people more than having to think.

—*Rev. Dr. Martin Luther King, Jr., civil rights activist and spiritual leader*

People demand freedom of speech as a compensation for freedom of thought, which they seldom use.

—Sóren Kierkegaard, philosopher

Everywhere I go I'm asked if I think the university stifles writers. My opinion is that they don't stifle enough of them.

—Flannery O'Connor, author

I have never let my schooling interfere with my education.

—Mark Twain, writer

I was thrown out of college for cheating on the metaphysics exam; I looked into the soul of the boy sitting next to me.

—*Woody Allen, filmmaker and actor*

I could work a mood better than anyone I knew. Unfortunately, the school had no accredited skulking program.

—*David Sedaris, writer*

Nothing we learn in this world is ever wasted.

—*Eleanor Roosevelt, social activist and U.S. First Lady*

Great Books

Outside of a dog, a book is a man's best friend.
Inside of a dog, it's too dark to read.

—*Groucho Marx, comedian*

What really knocks me out is a book that, when
you're all done reading it, you wish the author
that wrote it was a terrific friend of yours and
you could call him up on the phone whenever
you feel like it.

—*J. D. Salinger, writer*

Life-transforming ideas have always come to
me through books.

—*bell hooks, writer*

Every novel says to the reader, "Things are not as simple as you think."

—*Milan Kundera, writer*

You don't have to burn books to destroy a culture. Just get people to stop reading them.

—*Ray Bradbury, writer*

Masterpieces are not single and solitary births; they are the outcome of many years of thinking in common, of thinking by the body of the people, so that the experience of the mass is behind the single voice.

—*Virginia Woolf, writer*

A book is a version of the world. If you do not like it, ignore it; or offer your own version in return.

—*Salman Rushdie, writer*

A book must be an axe for the frozen sea inside of us.

—*Franz Kafka, writer*

Live a while in these books, learn from them what seems to you worth learning, but above all love them. This love will be repaid to you a thousand and a thousand times, and however your life may turn, it will, I am certain of it, run through the fabric of your growth.

—*Ranier Maria Rilke, poet*

People don't realize how a man's whole life can be changed by one book.

—Malcolm X, civil rights activist
and spiritual leader

What this town has not given her,
the book will provide...
The book has already lived through its troubles.
The book has a calm cover, a straight spine.

—Naomi Shihab Nye, poet

I have always imagined that paradise will be a kind of library.

—Jorge Luis Borges, writer

Problem-solving

You can tell whether a man is clever by his answers. You can tell whether a man is wise by his questions.

—*Naguib Mahfouz, writer*

Knowledge speaks, but wisdom listens.

—*Jimi Hendrix, musician*

The only interesting answers are those that destroy the questions.

—*Susan Sontag, writer and social activist*

Anyone who isn't confused really doesn't understand the situation.

—*Edward R. Murrow, journalist*

The test of a first-fate intelligence is the ability to hold two opposed ideas in mind at the same time and still retain the ability to function. One should, for example, be able to see that things are hopeless and yet be determined to make them otherwise.

—*F. Scott Fitzgerald, writer*

The mere formulation of a problem is far more essential than its solution, which may be merely a matter of mathematical or experimental skills. To raise new questions, new possibilities, to re-gard old problems from a new angle requires creative imagination and marks real advances in science.

—*Albert Einstein, physicist*

The beginning of knowledge is the discovery of something we do not understand.

—*Frank Herbert, writer*

Nothing in life is to be feared. It is only to be understood.

—*Marie Curie, scientist*

I've put in so many enigmas and puzzles that it will keep the professors busy for centuries arguing over what I meant … that's the only way of ensuring one's mortality.

—*James Joyce, writer*

The brain is like a muscle. When it is in use we feel very good. Understanding is joyous.

—*Carl Sagan, astrophysicist*

Enlightenment

As far as we can discern, the sole purpose of human existence is to kindle a light of meaning in the darkness of mere being.

—*Carl Gustav Jung, psychiatrist*

The ink of a scholar is more sacred than the blood of the martyr.

—*Prophet Muhammad, spiritual leader*

There is no purification in this world equal to wisdom.

—*from* Bhagavad Gita, *religious text*

Say not, "I have found the truth," but rather, "I have found a truth."

Say not, "I have found the path of the soul." Say rather, "I have met

the soul walking upon my path."

—*Khalil Gibran, poet*

Knowledge is indivisible. When people grow wise in one direction, they are sure to make it easier for themselves to grow wise in other directions as well.

—*Isaac Asimov, writer*

Wisdom is the supreme part of happiness.

—*Sophocles, writer*

It's not just learning things that's important. It's learning what to do with what you learn and learning why you learn things at all that matters.

—*Norton Juster, writer*

Learn at least this: What you are capable of. Let nothing stand in your way.

—*Tony Kushner, playwright*

Continuing Education

The true delight is in the finding out, rather than in the knowing.

—*Isaac Asimov, writer*

A mind that is stretched to a new idea never returns to its original dimension.

—*Oliver Wendell Holmes, writer*

You shall no longer take things at second or third hand, nor look through the eyes of the dead, nor feed on the specters in books; You shall not look through my eyes either, nor take things from me: You shall listen to all sides, and filter them from yourself.

—*Walt Whitman, poet*

I am always doing that which I cannot do, in order that I may learn how to do it.

—*Pablo Picasso, artist*

All truly wise thoughts have been thought already thousands of times; but to make them truly ours, we must think them over again honestly, till they take root in our personal experience.

—*Johann Wolfgang von Goethe, writer*

Never be afraid to sit awhile and think.

—*Lorraine Hansberry, playwright*

I find television very educating. The minute somebody turns it on, I go into the library and read a book.

—*Groucho Marx, comedian*

Dreams

Reality & Dreams

Everything you can imagine is real.

—*Pablo Picasso, artist*

Those who dream by day are cognizant of many things that escape those who dream only at night.

—*Edgar Allan Poe, writer*

He felt that his whole life was some kind of dream, and he sometimes wondered whose it was and whether they were enjoying it.

—*Douglas Adams, writer*

Nothing is as real as a dream. Responsibilities need not erase it. Duties need not obscure it. Because the dream is within you, no one can take it away.

—*Tom Clancy, writer*

Imagination and fiction make up more than three quarters of our real life.

—*Simone Weil, writer*

Who looks outside, dreams; who looks inside, awakes.

—*Carl Gustav Jung, psychiatrist*

A man is not what he thinks he is, but what he thinks, he is.

—*Jean Paul Sartre, philosopher*

You see things as they are and say, "Why?" But I dream things that never were and say, "Why not?"

—*George Bernard Shaw, writer*

Any map of the world without Utopia on it isn't even worth glancing at.

—*Oscar Wilde, playwright*

The dream is real, my friends. The failure to realize it is the only unreality.

—*Toni Cade Bambara, writer*

Creative Vision

A rock pile ceases to be a rock pile the moment
a single man contemplates it, bearing within
him the image of a cathedral.

—*Antoine de Saint-Exupéry, writer*

It is immaterial to me whether I run my ma-
chine in my mind or test it in my shop. The in-
ventions I have conceived in this way have
always worked. In thirty years there has not
been a single exception. My first electric motor,
the vacuum wireless light, my turbine engine
and many other devices have all been devel-
oped in exactly this way.

—*Nikola Tesla, inventor*

Fantasy, abandoned by reason, produces impossible monsters; united with it, she is the mother of the arts and the origin of marvels.

—*Francisco de Goya, artist*

Howls the sublime, and softly sleeps the calm ideal, in the whispering chambers of Imagination.

—*Charles Dickens, writer*

Like every writer, I am asked where my work originates, and if I knew I would go there more often.

—*Arthur Miller, playwright*

My dreams were all my own; I accounted for them to nobody; they were my refuge when annoyed—my dearest pleasure when free.

—*Mary Shelley, writer*

Ambition

If, after all, men cannot always make history have meaning, they can always act so that their own lives have one.

—*Albert Camus, writer*

Survival is the least of my desires.

—*Dorothy Allison, writer*

Lord, grant that I may always desire more than I can accomplish.

—*Michelangelo di Buonarotti, artist and architect*

None of us will ever accomplish anything excellent or commanding except when he listens to this whisper that is heard by him alone.

—*Ralph Waldo Emerson, writer*

Strive not to be a success, but rather to be of value.

—*Albert Einstein, physicist*

He knew what his aim was, because he had carried it hidden since infancy in an inviolable backwater of his heart.

—*Gabriel Garcia Marquez, writer*

I could clearly see the results of my labor: the long satin scarves and magazine covers were very real to me . . . The only crimp in my plan was that I seemed to have no talent whatsoever.

—*David Sedaris, writer*

Women who seek to be equal with men lack ambition.

—*Timothy Leary, writer*

Without leaps of imagination, or dreaming, we lose the excitement of possibilities. Dreaming, after all, is a form of planning.

—*Gloria Steinem, women's rights activist*

Be careful what you set your heart upon, for it will surely be yours.

—*James Arthur Baldwin, writer*

A man's reach should exceed his grasp.

—*Robert Browning, writer*

All our dreams can come true, if we have the courage to pursue them.

—*Walt Disney, animator and entrepreneur*

The most pitiful among men is he who turns his dreams into silver and gold.

—*Kahlil Gibran, poet*

It doesn't interest me what you do for a living. I want to know what you ache for, and if you dare to dream of meeting your heart's longing. It doesn't interest me how old you are. I want to know if you will risk looking like a fool for love, for your dream, for the adventure of being alive.

—*Oriah Mountain Dreamer, writer*

Pursuing Dreams

Hold fast to dreams, for if dreams die, life is a broken winged bird that cannot fly.

—*Langston Hughes, writer*

If you want to build a ship, don't drum up the men to gather wood, divide the work and give orders. Instead, teach them to yearn for the vast and endless sea.

—*Antoine de Saint-Exupéry, writer*

A dreamer is one who can find his way by moonlight, and see the dawn before the rest of the world.

—*Oscar Wilde, writer and playwright*

First they ignore you, then they laugh at you, then they fight you, then you win.

—*Mohandas K. Gandhi, politician and spiritual leader*

Far away there in the sunshine are my highest aspirations. I may not reach them, but I can look up and see their beauty, believe in them, and try to follow where they lead.

—*Louisa May Alcott, writer*

Stories were full of hearts being broken by love, but what really broke a heart was taking away its dream—whatever that dream might be.

—*Pearl S. Buck, writer*

Forget conventionalisms; forget what the world thinks of you stepping out of your place; think your best thoughts, speak your best words, do your best works, looking to your own conscience for approval.

—*Susan B. Anthony, women's rights activist*

In dreams begins responsibility.

—*William Butler Yeats, poet*

Ever tried. Ever failed. No matter. Try again. Fail again. Fail better.

—*Samuel Beckett, playwright*

If at first you don't succeed, try, try again. Then quit. There's no point in being a damn fool about it.

—*W. C. Fields, comedian*

Obstacles don't have to stop you. If you run into a wall, don't turn around and give up. Figure out how to climb it, go through it, or work around it.

—*Michael Jordon, athlete*

Learn the power of the trees. Let it flow. Let it go. That is the way you are going to make it through this storm.

—*Julia Butterfly Hill, environmentalist*

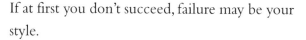

The hard and mighty shall fall; the flexible and yielding shall survive.

—*Lao Tzu, spiritual leader*

When life hands you a lemon, say, "Oh yeah, I like lemons. What else ya got?"

—*Henry Rollins, musician*

If at first you don't succeed, failure may be your style.

—*Quentin Crisp, writer*

You will do foolish things, but do them with enthusiasm.

—*Colette, writer*

People need trouble—a little frustration to sharpen the spirit on, toughen it.

—*William Faulkner, writer*

Don't let that horse
         eat that violin
cried Chagall's mother
But he
kept right on
painting

—*Lawrence Ferlinghetti, poet*

The world breaks everyone and afterward many
are strong at the broken places.

> —*Ernest Hemingway, writer*

Keeping the Faith

Dwell in possibility.

> —*Emily Dickinson, poet*

we take the thread of life
from the knots of darkness
tend the nursery of dreams
cool the burning sand
with shadows of palm trees

> —*Tawfiq Zayyad, poet*

Love not what you are, but what you may become.

— *Miguel de Cervantes, writer*

Dreams are the touchstones of our character.

— *Henry David Thoreau, philosopher*

Beware of allowing a tactless word, a rebuttal, a rejection to obliterate the whole sky.

— *Anaïs Nin, writer*

It's not the load that breaks you down, it's the way you carry it.

— *Lena Horne, musician*

Things never go so well that one should have no fear, and never so ill that one should have no hope.

—*Turkish proverb*

The fishermen know that the sea is dangerous and the storm terrible, but they have never found these dangers sufficient reasons for staying ashore.

—*Vincent Van Gogh, artist*

Faith is the bird that feels the light when the dawn is still dark.

—*Rabindranath Tagore, writer*

I have not failed. I've just found 10,000 ways that won't work.

—*Thomas Alva Edison, inventor*

There's a bit of magic in everything, and some loss to even things out.

—*Lou Reed, musician*

Life is a tragedy when seen in close-up, but a comedy in long-shot.

—*Charlie Chaplin, comedian*

In the midst of winter, I finally learned there was within me an invincible summer.

—*Albert Camus, writer*

We are all of us living in the gutter, but some of us are looking at the stars.

—*Oscar Wilde, playwright*

Dreams Realized

I rise
Into a daybreak that's wondrously clear
I rise
Bringing the gifts that my ancestors gave,
I am the dream and the hope of the slave.
I rise
I rise
I rise.

—*Maya Angelou, writer and educator*

There are victories of the soul and spirit. Sometimes, even if you lose, you win.

—*Eli Wiesel, writer and*
Holocaust survivor

You shall be free indeed not when your days are without a care nor your nights without a want and a grief,

But rather when these things girdle your life and yet you rise above them naked and unbound.

—*Khalil Gibran, poet*

As great scientists have said and as all children know, it is above all by the imagination that we achieve perception, and compassion, and hope.

—*Ursula K. LeGuin, writer*

Once you have tasted flight you will walk the earth with your eyes turned skywards, for there you have been and there you will long to return.

—*Leonard da Vinci, artist and inventor*

Planning

Introspection

Vision without action is a daydream. Action without vision is a nightmare.

—*Japanese proverb*

Your work is to discover your work and then with all your heart to give yourself to it.

—*Prince Gautama Siddharta (a.k.a. The Buddha), spiritual leader*

We all do "do, re, mi," but you have got to find the other notes yourself.

—*Louis Armstrong musician*

"Say, Pooh, why aren't you busy?" I said.
"Because it's a nice day," said Pooh.
"Yes, but—"
"Why ruin it?" he said.
"But you could be doing something Important," I said.
"I am," said Pooh.
"Oh? Doing what?"
"Listening," he said.

—*Benjamin Hoff, writer*

What lies behind us and what lies before us are small matters compared to what lies within us.

—*Ralph Waldo Emerson, writer*

You don't need a weatherman to know which way the wind blows.

—*Bob Dylan, musician*

There are as many ways to live as there are people on the earth and I shouldn't go around with blinkers but should see every way I can. Then I'll know what way I want to live and not just live like my family.

—*Louise Fitzhugh, writer*

The one thing that doesn't abide by majority rule is a person's conscience.

—*Harper Lee, writer*

The struggle has always been inner, and is played out on the outer terrains.

—*Gloria Anzaldúa, writer and activist*

If life becomes hard to bear, we think of a change in our circumstances. But the most important and effective change, a change in our own attitude, hardly ever occurs to us, and the resolution to take such a step is very difficult for us.

—*Ludwig Wittgenstein, philosopher*

When you have found your own room, be kind to those who have chosen different doors and to those who are still in the hall.

—*C. S Lewis, writer*

If you follow your bliss, doors will open for you that wouldn't have opened for anyone else.

—*Joseph Campbell, writer*

Charting a course

To think is easy. To act is hard. But the hardest thing in the world is to act in accordance with your thinking.

—*Johann Wolfgang von Goethe, writer*

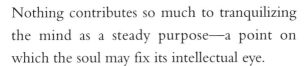

Nothing contributes so much to tranquilizing the mind as a steady purpose—a point on which the soul may fix its intellectual eye.

—*Mary Shelley, writer*

Never look down to test the ground before taking your next step; only he who keeps his eye fixed on the far horizon will find the right road.

—*Dag Hammarskjold,*
former U.N. Secretary-General

I have noticed even people who claim everything is predestined, and that we can do nothing to change it, look before they cross the road.

—*Steven Hawking, physicist*

Don't spend twenty years living your life by default when you can decide right now to go in the direction of your love. What do you really want?

—*Richard Bach, writer*

It is only by selection, by elimination, by emphasis that we get at the real meaning of things.

—*Georgia O'Keeffe, artist*

We never know how high we are
Till we are called to rise;
And then, if we are true to plan,
Our statures touch the skies.

—*Emily Dickinson, poet*

The possibilities are numerous once we decide to act and not react.

—*Gloria Anzaldúa, writer and social activist*

Do not be desirous of having things done quickly. Do not look at small advantages. Desire to have things done quickly prevents their being done thoroughly. Looking at small advantages prevents great affairs from being accomplished.

—Confucius, philosopher

It is not always by plugging away at a difficulty and sticking to it that one overcomes it; often it is by working on the one next to it. Some things have to be approached obliquely, at an angle.

—André Gide, writer

Life is what happens while you are making other plans.

—John Lennon, musician

You got to be careful if you don't know where you're going, because you might not get there.

—*Yogi Berra, sports figure*

One day Alice came to a fork in the road and saw a Cheshire cat in a tree. "Which road do I take?" she asked. "Where do you want to go?" was his response. "I don't know," Alice answered. "Then," said the cat, "it doesn't matter."

—*Lewis Carroll, writer*

When choosing between two evils, I always like to try the one I've never tried before.

—*Mae West, comedian*

Even if you're on the right track, you'll get run over if you just sit there.

—*Will Rogers, comedian*

It's good to have an end to journey toward; but it is the journey that matters, in the end.

—*Ursula K. LeGuin, writer*

Our goals can only be reached through a vehicle of a plan, in which we must fervently believe, and upon which we must vigorously act. There is no other route to success.

—*Pablo Picasso, artist*

Exploration

Make voyages. Attempt them. There's nothing else.

—*Tennessee Williams, playwright*

I'm an idealist. I don't know where I'm going, but I'm on my way.

—*Carl Sandburg, poet*

A good traveler has no fixed plans, and is not intent on arriving.

—*Lao Tzu, spiritual leader*

Not all who wander are lost.

—*J. R. R. Tolkien, writer*

I am open to the guidance of synchronicity, and do not let expectations hinder my path.

—*Dalai Lama, spiritual leader*

Life began in mystery, and it will end in mystery, but what a savage and beautiful country lies in between.

—*Diane Ackerman, writer*

Being twenty-something is all about taking it in: eating it, drinking it, and spitting out the seeds later ... It's about being in it, not on top of it.

—*Jodie Foster, filmmaker and actor*

I may not have gone where I intended to go, but I think I have ended up where I intended to be.

—*Douglas Adams, writer*

Without deviation, progress is not possible.

—*Frank Zappa, musician*

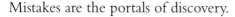

Mistakes are the portals of discovery.

—*James Joyce, writer*

If I must sail let it be on the ocean no matter how stormy—anything but a dull cruise on a level lake without ever losing sight of the same insipid shores by which it is surrounded.

—*Lord Byron, writer*

Life is a shipwreck, but we must not forget to sing in the lifeboats.

—*Voltaire, philosopher*

Towering genius disdains a beaten path. It seeks regions hitherto unexplored.

—*Abraham Lincoln, U.S. president*

Let us cut out
into stray eternity.
Somewhere the fields are full of larks.
Somewhere the land is swinging.

—*Lawrence Ferlinghetti, poet*

The real voyage of discovery consists not in seeking new landscapes but in having new eyes.

—*Marcel Proust, writer*

Wherever you go, go with all your heart.

—*Confucius, philosopher*

Effort

Seizing Opportunity

Opportunity is missed by most people because it is dressed in overalls and looks like work.

—Thomas Alva Edison, inventor

The winds of grace are always blowing, but it is you that must raise your sails.

—Rabindranath Tagore, writer

There is a tide in the affairs of men,
Which, taken at the flood, leads on to fortune;
Omitted, all the voyage of their life
Is bound in shallows and in miseries.

—*William Shakespeare, playwright and poet*

Life is a great big canvas, and you should throw all the paint on it you can.

—*Danny Kaye, actor and comedian*

Ever notice that "what the hell" is always the right decision?

—*Marilyn Munroe, comedian*

Opportunities multiply as they are seized.

—*Sun Tzu, philosopher*

To dare is to lose one's footing momentarily. Not to dare is to lose oneself.

—*Søren Kierkegaard, philosopher*

An ounce of application is worth a ton of abstraction.

—*Booker T. Washington, educator*
and civil rights activist

Must the hunger become anger and the anger fury before anything will be done?

—*John Steinbeck, writer*

Avoiding danger is no safer in the long run than outright exposure. The fearful are caught as often as the bold.

—*Helen Keller, educator*

We have to continually be jumping off cliffs and developing our wings on the way down.

—*Kurt Vonnegut, writer*

For of all sad words of tongue or pen,
The saddest are these: "It might have been!"

—*John Greenleaf Whittier, poet*

Life loves the liver of it.

—*Maya Angelou, writer and educator*

Donald heard a mermaid sing,
Susy spied an elf,
but all the magic I have known
I've had to make myself.

—*Shel Silverstein, poet*

I am a great believer in luck, and I find the harder I work, the more I have of it.

—*Thomas Jefferson, U.S. president*

Lying on a feather mattress or quilt will not bring you renown.

—*Leonardo da Vinci, artist and inventor*

Success usually comes to those who are too busy to be looking for it.

—*Henry David Thoreau, philosopher*

To hell with circumstances; I create oppor-tunities.

—*Bruce Lee, actor and athlete*

Things may come to those who wait, but only the things left by those who hustle.

—*Abraham Lincoln, U.S. president*

Procrastination

Every day for the last eighteen years he had got up in the morning with the intention of sorting out his career problem once and for all; as the day wore on, however, his burning desire to seek a place for himself in the outside world somehow got diminished.

—*Nick Hornby, writer*

Action is the antidote to despair.

—*Joan Baez, musician*

We all know the habit of cats of hesitating in an open doorway. Which of us has not said to a cat, "Well, come in if you want to"? There are men who, in moments when a decision is called for, hover uncertainly like the cat, at the risk of being crushed by the closing of the door. These cautious spirits may run greater risks than those who are more daring.

—*Victor Hugo, writer*

The years are flying past and we all waste so much time wondering if we dare to do this or that. The thing is to leap, to try, to take a chance.

—*Leonard Cohen, musician*

Only put off until tomorrow what you are willing to die having left undone.

—*Pablo Picasso, artist*

Too late, I found you can't wait to become perfect; you've got to go out and fall down and get up again with everybody else.

—*Ray Bradbury, writer*

Iron rusts from disuse, stagnant water loses its purity, and in cold weather becomes frozen: even so does inaction sap the vigors of the mind.

—*Leonardo Da Vinci, artist and inventor*

Vagueness and procrastination are ever a comfort to the frail in spirit.

—*John Updike, writer*

Time you enjoy wasting was not wasted.

—John Lennon, musician

It is better to have loafed and lost, than never to have loafed at all.

—James Thurber, cartoonist and writer

The world is filled with willing people: some willing to work, the rest willing to let them.

—Robert Frost, poet

A life spent making mistakes is not only more honorable but more useful than a life spent in doing nothing.

—George Bernard Shaw, writer

Believe me, you gotta get up early if you wanna get out of bed.

—*Groucho Marx, comedian*

Going Through the Motions

A life spent, however victoriously, in securing the necessaries of life is no more than an elaborate furnishing and decoration of apartments for the reception of a guest who is never to come. Our business here is not to live, but to live happily.

—*A. E. Housman, poet*

Expectations is the place you must always go to before you get to where you're going.
Of course, some people never go beyond Expectations ...

—*Norton Juster, writer*

Never keep up with the Joneses. Drag them down to your level.

—*Quentin Crisp, writer*

It is vain to say human beings ought to be satisfied with tranquility: they must have action; and they will make it if they cannot find it.

—*Charlotte Brontë, writer*

So we shall let the reader answer this question for himself: Who is the happier man, he who has braved the storm of life and lived, or he who has stayed securely on shore and merely existed?

—*Hunter S. Thompson, writer*

One ought, every day at least, to hear a little song, read a good poem, see a fine picture and, if possible, speak a few reasonable words.

—*Johann Wolfgang von Goethe, writer*

The trouble with the rat race is that even if you win, you're still a rat.

—*Lily Tomlin, comedian*

Once conform, do what other people do because they do it, and a lethargy steals over all the finer nerves and faculties of the soul. She becomes all outer show and inward emptiness; dull, callous, and indifferent.

—*Virginia Woolf, writer*

Most of life is so dull that there is nothing to be said about it, and the books and talk that would describe it as interesting are obliged to exaggerate, in the hope of justifying their own existence.

—*E.M. Forster, writer*

Any idiot can face a crisis. It's the day-to-day living that wears you out.

—*Anton Chekov, playwright*

Early to rise and early to bed makes a male healthy and wealthy and dead.

—*James Thurber, cartoonist and writer*

There is no time for cut-and-dried monotony. There is time for work. And time for love. That leaves no other time.

—*Coco Chanel, fashion designer*

Nothing is a waste of time if you use the experience wisely.

—*Auguste Rodin, sculptor*

Realizing Your Potential

Our deepest fear is not that we are inadequate. Our deepest fear is that we are power-ful beyond measure. It is our light, not our darkness, that most frightens us. We ask ourselves, who am I to be brilliant, gorgeous, talented and fabulous? Actually, who are you not to be? ... Your playing small doesn't serve the world. There's nothing enlightened about shrinking so that other people won't feel insecure around you ... as we let our own light shine, we unconsciously give other people permission to do the same. As we are liberated from our own fear, our presence automatically liberates others.

—*Nelson Mandela, former South African president (written by Marianne Williamson, writer)*

Everyone has inside of him a piece of good news. The good news is that you don't know how great you can be! How much you can love! What you can accomplish! And what your potential is!

—*Anne Frank, writer and Holocaust victim*

We must do that which we think we cannot.

—*Eleanor Roosevelt, social activist*
and U.S. First Lady

We take
unholy risks to prove
we are what we cannot be.

—*Leroi Jones/Imamu Amiri Baraka, poet*

Rise up ... you have nothing to lose but your chains.

—*Karl Marx, writer*

Always dream and shoot higher than you know you can do. Don't bother just to be better than your contemporaries or predecessors. Try to be better than yourself.

—*William Faulkner, writer*

Each of us must work for our own improvement and, at the same time, share a general responsibility for all humanity, our particular duty being to aid those to whom we think we can be most useful.

—*Marie Curie, scientist*

Be a lamp unto yourself. Work out your liberation with diligence.

—Prince Gautama Siddharta (a.k.a. The Buddha),
spiritual leader

It is better to die on your feet than to live on your knees!

—Emiliano Zapata, general and politican

There is a vitality, a life force, a quickening that is translated through you into action, and because there is only one of you in all time, this expression is unique. And if you block it, it will never exist through any other medium and be lost. The world will not have it.

—Martha Graham, dancer and choreographer

I'd rather be a failure at something I enjoy than a success at something I hate.

—*George Burns, comedian*

Many of life's failures are people who did not realize how close they were to success when they gave up.

—*Thomas Alva Edison, inventor*

However vast the darkness, we must supply our own light.

—*Stanley Kubrick, filmmaker*

If one is master of one thing and understands one thing well one has, at the same time, insight into and understanding of many things.

—*Vincent van Gogh, painter*

The artist is nothing without the gift, but the gift is nothing without work.

—*Emile Zola, writer*

The nature of the work is to prepare for a good accident.

—*Sidney Lumet, filmmaker*

We work in the dark—we do what we can—we give what we have. Our doubt is our passion and our passion is our task.

—*Henry James, writer*

Finish every day and be done with it. You have done what you could. Some blunders and absurdities crept in; forget them as soon as you can. Tomorrow is a new day; you shall begin it serenely and with too high a spirit to be encumbered with your old nonsense.

—*Ralph Waldo Emerson, writer*

Success

Accomplishments

I have learnt that success is to be measured not so much by the position that one has reached in life as by the obstacles which he has overcome while trying to succeed.

—*Booker T. Washington, educator and civil rights activist*

Our greatest glory is not in never falling, but in rising every time we fall.

—*Confucius, philosopher*

The real miracle is not to walk either on water or in thin air but to walk on earth.

—*Thich Nhat Hanh, spiritual leader*

It is not enough merely to exist. It's not enough to say, "I'm earning enough to support my family. I do my work well. I'm a good father, husband, churchgoer." That's all very well. But you must do something more ... Every man has to seek in his own way to realize his true worth. You must give some time to your fellow man. Even if it's a little thing, do something for those who need help, something for which you get no pay but the privilege of doing it. For remember, you don't live in a world all your own. Your brothers are here too.

—*Albert Schweitzer, writer and social activist*

Great things are done by a series of small things brought together.

—*Vincent van Gogh, painter*

We can do no great things; only small things with great love.

—*Mother Teresa, philanthropist and spiritual leader*

How far that little candle throws his beams!
So shines a good deed in a naughty world.

—*William Shakespeare, playwright and poet*

The key to immortality is first living a life worth remembering.

—*Saint Augustine of Hippo, spiritual leader*

Self-respect . . . cannot be purchased. It is never for sale . . . It comes to us when we are alone, in quiet moments, in quiet places, when we suddenly realize that, knowing the good, we have done it; knowing the beautiful, we have served it; knowing the truth, we have spoken it.

—*Noël Coward, songwriter*

To be yourself in a world that is constantly trying to make you something else is the greatest accomplishment.

—*Ralph Waldo Emerson, writer*

When you are content to be simply yourself and don't compare or compete, everybody will respect you.

—*Lao Tzu, spiritual leader*

It is not the mountain we conquer but our-selves.

> —*Sir Edmund Hillary, adventurer*

When you do the common things in life in an uncommon way, you will command the atten-tion of the world.

> —*George Washington Carver, writer*

Whatever I have devoted myself to, I have de-voted myself completely; in great aims and in small I have always thoroughly been in earnest.

> —*Charles Dickens, writer*

An excellent plumber is infinitely more admirable than an incompetent philosopher. The society which scorns excellence in plumbing because plumbing is a humble activity, and tolerates shoddiness in philosophy because it is an exalted activity, will have neither good plumbing nor good philosophy. Neither its pipes nor its theories will hold water.

—*John Gardner, writer*

If a man is called to be a street sweeper, he should sweep streets even as Michelangelo painted, or Beethoven composed music or Shakespeare wrote poetry. He should sweep streets so well that all the hosts of heaven and earth will pause to say, here lived a great street sweeper who did his job well.

—*Rev. Dr. Martin Luther King, Jr., civil rights activist and spiritual leader*

Fame

Fame is only good for one thing—they will cash your check in a small town.

—*Truman Capote, writer*

Worry not that no one knows of you; seek to be worth knowing.

—*Confucius, philosopher*

Since when was genius found respectable?

—*Elizabeth Barrett Browning, writer*

I started at the top and worked my way down.

—*Orson Welles, filmmaker*

Be not afraid of greatness; some are born great, some achieve greatness, and others have greatness thrust upon them.

—*William Shakespeare, playwright and poet*

Do good by stealth, and blush to find fame.

—*Alexander Pope, writer*

Modesty is a vastly overrated virtue.

—*John Kenneth Galbraith, writer*

I'm too fast. I'm too smart. I'm too pretty. I should be a postage stamp. That's the only way I'll ever get licked.

—*Muhammad Ali, athlete*

Being a hero is about the shortest-lived profession on earth.

—*Will Rogers, comedian*

Glory is fleeting, but obscurity is forever.

—*Napoleon Bonaparte, general and emperor*

I don't want to achieve immortality through my work . . . I want to achieve it through not dying.

—*Woody Allen, filmmaker and actor*

Dignity does not consist in possessing honors, but in deserving them.

—*Aristotle, philosopher*

We judge ourselves by what we feel capable of doing, while others judge us by what we have done.

—*Henry Wadsworth Longfellow, poet*

When everyone is somebody, then no one's anybody.

—*W. S. Gilbert, songwriter*

The public somebody you are when you have a "name" is a fiction ... The only somebody worth being is the solitary and unseen you that existed from your first breath and which is the sum of your actions and so is constantly in a state of becoming under your own volition—and knowing these things, you can even survive the catastrophe of Success.

—*Tennessee Williams, playwright*

Vanity asks the question—is it popular? Conscience asks the question—is it right?

—*Rev. Dr. Martin Luther King, Jr., civil rights activist and spiritual leader*

Outside show is a poor substitute for inner worth.

—*Aesop, writer*

It is not enough to succeed. Others must fail.

—*Gore Vidal, author*

We must believe in luck. For how else can we explain the success of those we don't like?

—*Jean Cocteau, author*

The penalty of success is to be bored by the people who used to snub you.

—*Nancy Astor, writer*

Achievement brings its own anticlimax.

—*Agatha Christie, author*

I dread success ... I like a state of continual becoming, with a goal in front and not behind.

—*George Bernard Shaw, writer*

To punish me for my contempt for authority, fate made me an authority myself.

—*Albert Einstein, physicist*

Ninety-eight percent of the adults in this country are decent, hard-working, honest Americans. It's the other lousy two percent that get all the publicity. But then—we elected them.

—*Lily Tomlin, comedian*

The growing good of the world is partly dependent on unhistoric acts; and that things are not so ill with you and me as they might have been, is half owing to the number who lived faithfully a hidden life, and rest in unvisited tombs.

—*George Eliot, writer*

Fortune

When the reviews are bad, I tell my staff they can join me as I cry all the way to the bank.

—*Liberace, musician*

It is a funny thing about life; if you refuse to accept anything but the best you very often get it.

—*William Somerset Maugham, writer*

I used to think I was poor. Then they told me I wasn't poor, I was needy. Then they told me it was self-defeating to think of myself as needy. I was deprived. (Oh, not deprived, but rather underprivileged.) Then they told me that underprivileged was overused. I was disadvantaged. I still don't have a dime. But I have a great vocabulary.

—*Jules Feiffer, cartoonist*

Everything in the world may be endured except continued prosperity.

—*Johann Wolfgang von Goethe, writer*

There must be more to life than having every-thing.

—*Maurice Sendak, writer*

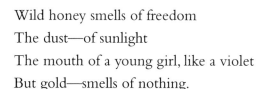

Wild honey smells of freedom
The dust—of sunlight
The mouth of a young girl, like a violet
But gold—smells of nothing.

—*Anna Akhmatova, poet*

Possessions, outward success, publicity, luxury—to me these have always been contemp-tible. I believe that a simple and unassuming manner of life is best for everyone, best for both the body and the mind.

—*Albert Einstein, physicist*

Money can't buy you happiness, but it can buy you a yacht big enough to pull up right alongside it.

—*David Lee Roth, musician*

The Pursuit of Happiness

How do you measure success? To laugh often, and much; to win the respect of intelligent people and the affection of children; to earn the appreciation of honest critics and endure the betrayal of false friends; to appreciate beauty; to find the best in others; to leave the world a bit better, whether by a healthy child, a redeemed social condition, or a job well done; to know even one other life has breathed because you lived—this is to have succeeded.

—*Ralph Waldo Emerson, writer*

A man is a success if he gets up in the morning and gets to bed at night, and in between he does what he wants to do.

—*Bob Dylan, musician*

The ultimate of being successful is the luxury of giving yourself the time to do what you want to do.

—*Leontyne Price, musician*

I am independent! I can live alone and I love to work.

—*Mary Cassatt, artist*

No artist is ever pleased … [there is no] satisfaction whatever at any time. There is only a queer, divine dissatisfaction, a blessed unrest that keeps us marching and makes us more alive than the others.

—Martha Graham, dancer and choreographer

Maybe we all live life at too high a pitch, those of us who absorb emotional things all day, and as a consequence we can never feel merely content: we have to be unhappy, or ecstatically, head-over-heels happy, and those states are difficult to achieve within a stable, solid relationship.

—Nick Hornby, writer

If only we'd stop trying to be happy we'd have a pretty good time.

—Edith Wharton, writer

Sooner or later in life everyone discovers that perfect happiness is unrealizable, but there are few who pause to consider the antithesis: that perfect unhappiness is equally unattainable.

—*Primo Levi, writer*

Clouds come floating into my life, no longer to carry rain or usher storm, but to add color to my sunset sky.

—*Rabindranath Tagore, writer*

We do have a zeal for laughter in most situations, give or take a dentist.

—*Joseph Heller, writer*

You gotta love livin', baby, 'cause dyin' is a pain in the ass!

—*Frank Sinatra, musician*

Happiness is a butterfly which when pursued, is always just beyond our grasp, but which if you will sit down quietly, may alight upon you.

—*Nathianiel Hawthorne, writer*

Most men pursue pleasure with such breathless haste that they hurry past it.

—*Sóren Kierkegaard, philosopher*

Life itself is the proper binge.

—*Julia Child, chef*

Happiness always looks small while you hold it in your hands, but let it go, and you learn at once how big and precious it is.

—*Maxim Gorky, writer*

Let us so live that when we come to die even the undertaker will be sorry.

—*Mark Twain, writer*

The ones for me are the mad ones, the ones who are mad to live, mad to talk, mad to be saved, desirous of everything at the same time, who never yawn or say a commonplace thing, but burn, burn, burn like fabulous yellow roman candles exploding like spiders across the stars.

—*Jack Kerouac, writer*

Friendship

Forming Bonds

Cultivating a close, warmhearted feeling for others automatically puts the mind at ease. It helps remove whatever fears or insecurities we may have and gives us the strength to cope with any obstacles we encounter. It is the principal source of success in life.

—*Dalai Lama, spiritual leader*

There is nothing more truly artistic than to love people.

—*Vincent Van Vogh, artist*

To cement a new friendship, especially between foreigners or persons of a different social world, a spark with which both were secretly charged must fly from person to person, and cut across the accidents of place and time.

—*Cornelia Otis Skinner, writer*

It's a form of love just to talk to somebody that you have nothing in common with and still be fascinated by their presence.

—*David Byrne, musician*

Love is the only force capable of transforming an enemy into friend.

—*Rev. Dr. Martin Luther King, Jr., civil rights activist and spiritual leader*

Kind words can be short and easy to speak, but their echoes are truly endless.

—*Mother Teresa, philanthropist and spiritual leader*

The bird a nest the spider a web the human friendship.

—*William Blake, writer and artist*

A friend may well be reckoned the masterpiece of nature.

—*Ralph Waldo Emerson, writer*

Each friend represents a world in us, a world possibly not born until they arrive, and it is only by this meeting that a new world is born.

—*Anaïs Nin, writer*

No one would choose a friendless existence on condition of having all the other things in the world.

—*Aristotle, philosopher*

Friendship is unnecessary, like philosophy, like art ... It has no survival value; rather it is one of those things that give value to survival.

—*C. S. Lewis, writer*

Nobody, but nobody
Can make it out here alone.

—*Maya Angelou, writer and educator*

If you haven't learned the meaning of friendship, you really haven't learned anything.

—*Muhammad Ali, athlete*

Savor kindness, because cruelty is always possible later.

—*Jenny Holzer, artist*

Where there is great love there are always miracles.

—*Willa Cather, writer*

In everyone's life, at some time, our inner fire goes out. It is then burst into flame by an encounter with another human being. We should be thankful for those people who rekindle the inner spirit.

—*Albert Schweitzer, writer and social activist*

Let us be grateful to people who make us happy; they are the charming gardeners who make our souls blossom.

—*Marcel Proust, writer*

I am a kind of paranoiac in reverse. I suspect people of plotting to make me happy.

—*J. D. Salinger, writer*

When you have once seen the glow of happiness on the face of a beloved person, you know that a man can have no vocation but to awaken that light on the faces surrounding him.

—*Albert Camus, writer*

Understanding

Friendship is a single soul dwelling in two bodies.

—Aristotle, philosopher

One grows accustomed to being praised, or being blamed, or being advised, but it is unusual to be understood.

—E. M. Forster, writer

The sharing of joy, whether physical, emotional, psychic, or intellectual, forms a bridge between the sharers which can be the basis for understanding much of what is not shared between them.

—Audre Lorde, writer

It is not our purpose to become each other; it is to recognize each other, to learn to see the other and honor him for what he is.

—*Hermann Hesse, writer*

Perhaps the most delightful friendships are those in which there is much agreement, much disputation, and yet more personal liking.

—*George Eliot, writer*

I don't need a friend who changes when I change and who nods when I nod; my shadow does that much better.

—*Plutarch, writer*

We are the night ocean filled
with glints of light. We are the space
between the fish and the moon,
while we sit here together.

—Rumi, spiritual leader

The language of friendship is not words but
meanings.

—Henry David Thoreau, philosopher

Those truly linked don't need correspondence.
When they meet again after many years apart,
their friendship is as true as ever.

—Deng Ming-Dao, writer

True friends are two people who are comfort-able sharing silence together.

—*Ralph Waldo Emerson, writer*

The illusion that we are separate from one an-other is an optical delusion of our conscious-ness.

—*Albert Einstein, physicist*

how do you write a poem
about someone so close
to you that when you say ahhhhh
they say chuuuu

—*Nikki Giovanni, writer*

Loyalty

We are each other's harvest; we are each other's business; we are each other's magnitude and bond.

—*Gwendolyn Brooks, writer*

A faithful friend is a strong defense: and he that hath found such a one hath found a treasure.

—*From the Bible, Ecclesiasticus 6:14*

It's the friends you can call up at 4 a.m. that matter.

—*Marlene Dietrich, actor*

You may forget the one with whom you have laughed, but never the one with whom you have wept.

—*Khalil Gibran, poet*

It is one of the blessings of old friends that you can afford to be stupid with them.

—*Ralph Waldo Emerson, writer*

Lots of people want to ride with you in the limo, but what you want is someone who will take the bus with you when the limo breaks down.

—*Oprah Winfrey, actor, filmmaker, and entrepreneur*

True friendship is a plant of slow growth, and must undergo and withstand the shocks of adversity before it is entitled to the appellation.

—*George Washington, U.S. president*

He remembers his friends
and forgives them their taunts.
He laughs
and releases all his birds into the fog.

—*'Ali Ja'far al-'Allaq, poet*

I have friends in overalls whose friendship I would not swap for the favor of the kings of the world.

—*Thomas Alva Edison, inventor*

Champagne to my real my friends, and real pain to my sham friends.

—*Tom Waits, musician*

Goodbyes

Nothing makes the earth seem so spacious as to have friends at a distance: they make the latitudes and longitudes.

—*Henry David Thoreau, philosopher*

Where you used to be, there is a hole in the world, which I find myself constantly walking around in the daytime and falling into at night.

—*Edna St. Vincent Millay, poet*

Never shall I forget the days I spent with you. Continue to be my friend, as you will always find me yours.

—*Ludwig van Beethoven, musician*

Look as long as you can at the friend you love,
No matter whether that friend is moving away
   from you
Or coming back toward you.

—*Rumi, spiritual leader*

Every exit is ...an entrance someplace else.

—*Tom Stoppard, playwright*

The road to a friend's house is never long.

—*Danish Proverb*

Old friends pass away, new friends appear. It is just like the days. An old day passes, a new day arrives. The important thing is to make it meaningful: a meaningful friend—or a meaningful day.

—*Dalai Lama, spiritual leader*

You're gonna have to leave me now I know
But I'll look for you in the sky above
In the tall grass, in the ones I love
You're gonna make me lonesome when you go

—*Bob Dylan, musician*

Love is the only thing that we can carry with us when we go.

—*Louisa May Alcott, writer*

Transitions

The Future

There is a dreamlike quality to every commencement day ...You stand at a boundary. Behind you is your natural habitat, as it were, the ground of your creaturely being, the old haunts where you were nurtured; in front of you is a less knowable prospect of invitation and challenge, the testing ground of your possibilities. You stand between whatever binds you to your past and whatever might be unbounded in your future.

—*Seamus Heaney, poet*

What do I know of man's destiny? I could tell you more about radishes.

—*Samuel Beckett, playwright*

We are made wise not by the recollection of our past, but by the responsibility for our future.

—*George Bernard Shaw, writer*

What's past is prologue.

—*William Shakespeare, playwright and poet*

In this world, there's a kind of painful progress. Longing for what we've left behind, and dreaming ahead.

—*Tony Kushner, playwright*

I like the dreams of the future better than the history of the past.

— *Thomas Jefferson, U.S. president*

Tomorrow is the mysterious, unknown guest.

— *Henry Wadsworth Longfellow, poet*

The future perfect I have always regarded as an oxymoron.

— *Tom Stoppard, playwright*

There is no smooth road into the future: but we go round, or scramble over the obstacles. We've got to live, no matter how many skies have fallen.

— *D. H. Lawrence, writer*

When I despair, I remember that all through history the way of truth and love have always won. There have been tyrants, and murderers, and for a time they can seem invincible, but in the end they always fall. Think of it ... always.

—*Mohandas K. Gandhi, politician and spiritual leader*

The world is before you, and you need not take it or leave it as it was before you came in.

—*James Arthur Baldwin, writer*

The only thing that makes life possible is permanent, intolerant uncertainty: not knowing what comes next.

—*Ursula LeGuin, writer*

The caged bird sings
with a fearful trill
of things unknown
but longed for still

—*Maya Angelou, writer and educator*

Time, when it is left to itself and no definite demands are made on it, cannot be trusted to move at any recognized pace. Usually it loiters; but just when one has come to count upon its slowness, it may suddenly break into a wild irrational gallop.

—*Edith Wharton, writer*

Time sneaks up on you like a windshield on a bug.

—*John Lithgow, actor*

I never think of the future. It comes soon enough.

—*Albert Einstein*

Living in the Moment

We touch the moment
with our fingers,
we cut it
to size,
we direct its blooming.
It's living, it's alive:
It brings nothing from yesterday that can't be redeemed

—*Pablo Neruda, poet*

There is never time in the future in which we will work out our salvation. The challenge is in the moment; the time is always now.

—*James Arthur Baldwin, writer*

The past and the future happen at the present moment.

—*Rick Moody, writer*

Oh, I've had my moments, and if I had to do it all over again, I'd have many more of them. In fact I'd try not to have anything else, just moments, one after another, instead of living so many years ahead of my day.

—*Jorge Luis Borges, writer*

In the end it's not the years in your life that count. It's the life in your years.

—*Abraham Lincoln, U.S. president*

Light tomorrow with today!

—*Elizabeth Barrett Browning, writer*

If my doctor told me I had only six minutes to live, I wouldn't brood. I'd type a little faster.

—*Isaac Asimov, writer*

Twenty years from now you will be more disappointed by the things you didn't do than by the ones you did. So throw off the bowlines. Sail away from the safe harbor. Catch the trade winds in your sails. Explore. Dream.

—*Mark Twain, writer*

Here we are, trapped in the amber of the moment. There is no why.

—*Kurt Vonnegut, writer*

Without realizing it, the individual composes his life according to the laws of beauty even in times of greatest distress.

—*Milan Kundera, writer*

Have patience with everything that remains unsolved in your heart … At present you need to live the question. Perhaps you will gradually, without even noticing it, find yourself experiencing the answer, some distant day.

—*Rainer Maria Rilke, poet*

Let us not look back in anger, nor forward in fear, but around in awareness.

—*James Thurber, cartoonist and writer*

Transformation

When old words die out on the tongue, new melodies break forth from the heart; and where the old tracks are lost, new country is revealed with its wonders.

—*Rabindranath Tagore, writer*

It's a good thing to have all the props pulled out from under us occasionally. It gives us some sense of what is rock under our feet, and what is sand.

—*Madeleine L'Engle, writer*

Without change, something sleeps inside us, and seldom awakens. The sleeper must awaken.

—*Frank Herbert, writer*

Restlessness and discontent are the first necessities of progress.

—*Thomas Alva Edison, inventor*

Change everything, except your passions.

—*Voltaire, philosopher*

They must often change, who would be constant in happiness or wisdom.

—*Confucius, philosopher*

Human beings, by change, renew, rejuvenate ourselves; otherwise we harden.

—*Johann Wolfgang von Goethe, writer*

It is not the strongest of the species that survive, nor the most intelligent, but the one most responsive to change.

—*Charles Darwin, scientist*

And these children that you spit on
as they try to change their world
are immune to your consultations
They're quite aware
of what they're going through
Changes …

—*David Bowie, musician*

The ultimate measure of a man is not where he stands in moments of comfort and convenience, but where he stands at times of challenge and controversy.

—*Rev. Dr. Martin Luther King, Jr., civil rights activist and spiritual leader*

Not everything that is faced can be changed, but nothing can be changed until it is faced.

—*James Arthur Baldwin, writer*

Change is not merely necessary to life. It is life.

—*Alvin Toffler, writer*

When the going gets weird, the weird turn pro.

—*Hunter S. Thompson, writer*

It is change, continuing change, inevitable change, that is the dominant factor in society today. No sensible decision can be made any longer without taking into account not only the world as it is, but the world as it will be.

—*Isaac Asimov, writer*

Life isn't one straight line. Most of us have to be transplanted, like a tree, before we blossom.

—*Louise Nevelson, artist*

Changing the World

We see the brightness of a new page where everything yet can happen.

—*Rainer Maria Rilke, poet*

One thing I know: the only ones among you who will be really happy are those who will have sought and found how to serve.

—*Albert Schweitzer, writer and social activist*

We are here on earth to do good for others. What the others are here for, I don't know.

—*W. H. Auden, poet*

Waste no more time arguing about what a good man should be. Be one.

—*Marcus Aurelius, emperor*

Only those who bear its burdens may rightfully enjoy the blessings of civilized society.

—*Eugene V. Debs, politician*

It is not what we do, but also what we do not do, for which we are accountable.

—*Molière, actor and playwright*

All labor that uplifts humanity has dignity and importance and should be undertaken with painstaking excellence.

—*Rev. Dr. Martin Luther King, Jr., civil rights activist and spiritual leader*

The changes in our life must come from the impossibility to live otherwise than according to the demands of our conscience ... not from our mental resolution to try a new form of life.

—*Leo Tolstoy, writer*

Be not simply good; be good for something.

—*Henry David Thoreau, philosopher*

They say that time changes things, but you actually have to change them yourself.

—*Andy Warhol, artist*

Any form of art is a form of power, it has impact, it can affect change—it cannot only move us, it makes us move.

—*Ossie Davis, writer*

Every morning I wake torn between a desire to save the world and an inclination to savor it. This makes it hard to plan the day.

—*E. B. White, writer*

It is almost as if you were frantically construct-ing another world while the world that you live in dissolves beneath your feet, and that your survival depends on completing this construc-tion at least one second before the old habita-tion collapses.

—*Tennessee Williams, playwright*

You must be the change you wish to see in the world.

—*Mohandas K. Gandhi, politician*
and spiritual leader

In a world where there is so much to be done, I felt strongly impressed that there must be something for me to do.

—*Dorthea Dix, social activist*

Although the world is full of suffering, it is also full of the overcoming of it.

—*Helen Keller, educator*

Beginnings

Whatever you can do, or dream you can, begin it. Boldness has genius, power and magic in it.

—*Johann Wolfgang von Goethe, writer*

How wonderful it is that nobody need wait a single moment before starting to improve the world.

—*Anne Frank, writer and Holocaust victim*

Man cannot discover new oceans unless he has the courage to lose sight of the shore.

—*André Gide, writer*

It is never too late to be what you might have been.

—*George Eliot, writer*

The world is a book, and those who stay at home read only one page.

—*St. Augustine of Hippo, spiritual leader*

Courage …is when you know you're licked before you begin, but you begin anyway and you see it through no matter what.

—*Harper Lee, writer*

Start where you are. Use what you have. Do what you can.

—*Arthur Ashe, athlete*

There are two mistakes one can make along the road to truth ... not going all the way, and not starting.

—*Prince Gautama Siddharta (a.k.a. The Buddha), spiritual leader*

It is not death that man should fear, but never beginning to live.

—*Marcus Aurelius, emperor*

"Begin at the beginning," the King said, gravely, "and go on till you come to the end; then stop."

—*Lewis Carroll, author*